Crossroads of Love

Crossroads of Love
Author:
Lisa Marie Dominguez

Thank you to my wonderful family and my children for understanding my journey and allowing me to write this book in my time.

This book is a fictional book that allows us to walk in the shoes of many abused woman. I ask you to read this and understand why so many women put themselves in so many bad situations after the abuse.

Abuse comes in many different forms. It can be mental or physical abuse, even in the form of neglect.

Abuse causes soul searching, to look for that one person that they can trust but at the same time they do not feel worthy, all the while misunderstanding why they go through such internal torment.

Rise up above and see that everyone is beautiful and deserves to be loved the right way!

Find your forever and remove all the time beings from your life! You are worth it….

This is for all the women that have felt lost at one time

Contents

Chapter one
   running away

Chapter two
   making all the wrong choices

Chapter three
   empty love

Chapter four
   finally healing

Introduction

I decided to write this book as a part of healing. If you have been a victim of physical and emotional abuse you will clearly understand the need to get away from your inner self. To heal your soul, to live in a fantasy and that is exactly what this book does, it takes you away to the fantasy of a woman running away, experiencing life and taking chances, through making all the wrong choices but ending up with what she has deserved all along.

The process of her journey is the inner torment of emotional abuse, everyone that has been through anything like this knows at one time or another you will have to take full responsibility for all the wrong roads that you took, the decisions you made, the time lost, and the lessons learned.

By the end of this story you can see where the journey took Lizzy and you will experience all the healing through reading this *adult* book.

Live life in fantasy and read my book. Take yourself away from your torment and heal through this journey. You will feel yourself relating to Lizzy as she struggles through the pain, through the torment, through the unknown, through the heartache, all the questions and the uncertainties. The lust, the intimacy, the wrong choices, getting taken advantage of and finally turning her life around. In the end you will learn and know that everything will be okay in your life as well.

Let your mind experience this book, to understand it and to feel each word, each message, each let down. Follow Lizzy until she realizes in the end that she was self-destructing and discovers the final destination to her life. We will and can get there if we leave the pain behind and understand it's up to us to love ourselves and release it.

When we carry pain, we allow others to take full advantage of us, of our kindness and of our nature to please others to feel accepted and desired. Remove that from who you are, begin the healing and love yourself. Remember that self gratification through all the wrong things only hurts you more and it lasts for such a small amount of time.

So absolutely love yourself, free your soul, move forward, and live your life for yourself. To forgive is to heal and live freely.

Author,

Lisa Marie Dominguez

This is a story about a small town, beautiful, innocent young woman with many dreams and desires. She made sure they came true; she was tired of walking the straight line and walked right into a maze. The maze of life...

Chapter One

One hot summer day Lizzy's emotions exploded with desire to run away from everything she knew. She ran to the nearest bus station with so many emotions of frustration, excitement, and fear that left her heart racing. All she kept thinking was whether she was making the right choice. Everything in her said, "YES!"

Lizzy was a good wholesome girl, she always did the right thing and made all the right choices. Her grandparents raised her in a little town where everyone knew each other closely. She did not have a good relationship with her mother and she had no idea or desire to know who her father was. Lizzy's mother never stuck to one man and probably wouldn't be able to identify her father anyway. When her mother visited from the Big City she never came empty handed and it was never with the same man.

Lizzy never cared to know or understand her mother, they were very different, so she thought. She loved being an only child and having the privacy that her grandparents gave her. She was embarrassed of the choices her mother made with men and the way the town talked about her. The only memories Lizzy had of her mother weren't pleasant. Her grandparents were very old now and she always did the right thing to prevent hurting them like her mother.

In elementary school, Lizzy was a tough girl and had many friends. The town was so small that it seemed like one big happy family. Lizzy never paid attention to the infatuation game that her friends played. She could never see herself falling in love with one of her friends that she considered a buddy.

When Lizzy past to junior high school, things didn't seem to change, she still had the same friends. But, Lizzy passed everyone up when it came to puberty. By her 8th grade year she looked like a stunning young woman. Her body had already started to develop, leaving her friends behind. This made Lizzy uncomfortable, since she had no one to explain what was happening to her. She wore big clothing so that no one would know that her breast had reached the voluptuous size of a C cup.

Lizzy's grandparents were very loving, but they didn't give her the attention she required or needed at her age. Lizzy had no one to teach her about life, about puberty, sex or even her menstrual cycle. She couldn't turn to her mother for advice out of fear that it wasn't the advice she wanted to know. She couldn't handle turning to her mother for anything. Not even to help her understand her emotions or the changes her body had started going through.

In school she stained her white shorts. She had no idea what was happening to her body. She skipped her class and went to the nurse very scared. The nurse handed her a pack of pads and explained that she was going through puberty. She told Lizzy about her period and the changes her body would be going through and forewarned her with a long lecture about not having sex. Lizzy was very scared and didn't understand anything about getting pregnant, sex and how they related to her period. She just could not image herself with a boyfriend now! Lizzy was embarrassed after the long conversation with her school nurse and felt very sick from cramping that she up skipping school for the rest of the day. She didn't even bother telling her grandmother about her experience or how she felt. Lizzy didn't realize this thing that she was going through was normal, she isolated and couldn't tell her friends.

In high school she was very active with social clubs and sports. She became very popular because of her intelligence and friendliness. Her classmates did not realize how beautiful Lizzy really was because she hid behind large clothing that hid her shape.

She had a large range of friends in high school. Lizzy talked to the kickers, and the sex fanatic girls that told stories in detail as Lizzy listened with fascination and fear. She had one friend that considered himself a punk rocker, with dyed, flaming red hair. Juan went to visit family in the city for the summer and came back with some bad city habits. Then, there were the cool, rockers. She enjoyed the same music they did. It always seemed to take her far away from all the uncertainty in her mind. Lizzy's grandparent's land was 10 acres and she loved to invite friends over to hang out far back in the yard by a big Oak tree. Lizzy let the music embrace her mind of all the possibilities. She always closed her eyes and imagined herself in another place.

Each year the small town had a festival with carnival rides and all her friends would get together at her grandparents' home and sit on the big wooden porch that was off the main street. They would light candle lanterns and line the sidewalks. They all sat around and watched the long line of cars come in. Many of the people from the city would drive in for the festival. Lizzy dreamt each year that she would meet someone from the city, but never got the nerve to even go to the festival after she entered high school. It was the same excuse each year, she never wanted to leave her grandparents alone with so many strangers in town. Lizzy remembered all the rides, games, food and the sweet smell of fun. Her friends begged her to come listen to the bands, they knew music was her favorite thing. But, year after year Lizzy just admired the people from afar in the comfort of her home.

Lizzy started to day dream about what it would be like to love someone and to be loved. All her friends started to talk more about leaving to college right after graduation. Yet, Lizzy was too afraid to leave her grandparents, they were very old and not in good health. There were no colleges in her small town so if she planned to go to college, she knew she must move and that scared her away from furthering her education. Lizzy started to work for the town thrift store part time while she was a senior in high school. She graduated 7 days after her 18th birthday and as expected graduation came and went. Everyone left for college or to explore the world. But, Lizzy on the other hand decided to stay and continue working part time. Her grandparents had grown very sick and her mother started to visit more often. They had to hire someone to come into the home and help her grandparents. This made Lizzy feel helpless and afraid.

To Lizzy, life was going by in slow motion and it seemed like the day after graduation to her. But it wasn't and three years had passed quickly. She was still working part time and taking care of her grandparents on her free time. Her friends would visit and try to encourage her to leave, but she wasn't ready. And every time her mother would come by the house, Lizzy felt that her mother was just intruding. She just hated those days as they became more frequent. She felt that her mother only came for money.

Her grandparents did well and promised to leave Lizzy everything. She would be getting the house, the land, the cars every cent and everything they carried under their names. The last person she wanted taking anything was her dysfunctional mother. Besides, what had her mother ever done for her grandparents anyway other than hurt them?

That dreadful day came, she received a call at work from her mother informing her that her grandmother took her last breath. Lizzy took time off to help with the funeral. Her first call was to her grandmother's youngest sister, Auntie Jane and she helped Lizzy inform everyone in the family about the funeral arrangements. There were so many relatives in her home that she had never met. They all welcomed her to come visit them in the city but as always, she turned them away finding some excuse.

At grandmother's funeral, everyone said that grandfather would pass soon after, and he did. They loved each other for a lifetime, how could he have lived without her? That's the kind of love that Lizzy wanted to find. She wanted it to last a lifetime. She would always remember all the great stories that her grandmother shared with her. Lizzy enjoyed hearing how her grandparents met in school and knew they were meant to be. Her grandmother always told the story of their first kiss and how they held hands as the music brought them together. She would sing as grandfather played the guitar. After they married, they would cook together and took long walks and laughed lying in the grass. Lizzy closed her eyes as she lays in bed thinking about how she wanted that so bad.

Several weeks after everything calmed down and

her Aunt Jane finally went home from grandfather's funeral, Lizzy felt anxious. She felt a burning feeling inside her to run away. She ran upstairs and turned the cold water on. As the cold water hit her body, she screamed as loud as she could. She was frustrated feeling out of control with sadness and uncertainty. She was already late for work, so she dressed in a rush as her mind and body told her not to. She walked out the door with her hair still wet and pulled back, she never wore makeup and nothing she had needed ironing, she was ready in no time.

Lizzy entered the thrift store where she had worked for three years now. She kept thinking that she couldn't do it, she couldn't spend another day in that store with those boring people. It bothered Lizzy because she knew she was just like them. They had no meaning to their lives, they would never become anything or anybody. She felt anxious inside, she felt the need to run, to run away and do something wild, to have stories of her own.

Lizzy paced back and forth and thought to herself that she just couldn't unpack another box of old used up things that people brought in daily. She couldn't focus, all she wanted to do was run. She needed to feel wanted, to feel loved, but she felt so alone. She turned to the door and there he stood her best friend from high school. She never realized how attractive Bill was as they stood eye to eye. His hair was light brown, kind of shaggy, his eyes were a deep brown, and his skin was sunburned from working on his dad's farm. As Bill stood in front of her at the door, Lizzy noticed his full lips. Bill started to say hi to her as she walked up to him and slowly put her hand on his mouth, covering it to prevent words. He looked at her confused but stepped back and walked past her. She thought she could do it but couldn't. She couldn't bring herself to kiss him, even though she felt it, in her mind she felt it was so wrong.

Lizzy refused to clock in as she continued to pace. She had her car parked out front and her purse still strapped over her shoulder. She thought that maybe she should just go home for the day. But what would that solve? Bill came back to check on her, he asked her if she was okay, but she had no words as she stood there feeling anxious. Finally, she opened her purse, pulled out her keys and threw them to him. Then she yelled out, "Take my car home for me!" Lizzy knew what she needed to do, she needed to leave that old town that held her back, the town that made her the pure 21 year old woman that she was today.

Lizzy ran without looking back, without stopping. She ran until she reached the bus station that was several blocks away from the thrift store in town where she worked. Who cares where the train would take her, she thought, as long as it's away from here. She had all the money she needed. Her grandparents left her well off, she had no worries. She paced back and forth, out of breath, thinking as she looked at the destinations and departure times.

"That's it! That's where I want to be!" she told the man at the ticket station. Lizzy heard so many stories about this place, many unspeakable things. She was on her way to The Party City! She was scared as she entered the bus, but it was what she wanted, what she desired, to experience life. Her heart was racing with excitement as she handed the bus driver her departure ticket. This was a feeling she had never felt before, she felt excited. But, was it the right thing? She kept thinking, whether she was making the right choice and everything in her said "YES!"

As the bus departed, she felt a sense of relief and then a sense of fear. Not knowing where she would stay, where she would work, how would she get around? It scared her but the more she felt scared, the more she wanted this.

As the bus drove off, she felt more and more nervous. She kept thinking of her grandparents and how she missed them so much. Lizzy thought maybe she was in mourning and that's why her mind was so mixed up, but then again, she had these feelings before her grandparents past away.

How was it that she hid these feelings for so long? She wanted to know what it was like to live on her own, to meet people so different, and to make love to a man. She always told herself that she would never be like her mother, and that she would wait until she found the right man then fall in love and get married. But, what if that day never came what if she never found Mr. Right, like grandma did? She wanted to know what the big deal was about sex, thinking back to when her junior high school nurse scared her with a lecture. What if it wasn't all that great? She could never go back, once it's done that's it, it's done.

She finally felt calm and rested for a short time until the bus made its first stop. The bus driver announced that he would be stopping for 30 minutes. Everyone departed the bus, but Lizzy's mind was too drained, too tired to instruct her body to move. She closed her eyes and went back to sleep. Everyone entered the bus for departure. Lizzy didn't realize that other people would be entering and exiting the bus periodically as the trip went on. The bus ride seemed to get increasingly uncomfortable for Lizzy. She started to feel like a sardine, she needed air. At the next stop, Lizzy decided to get off the bus so that she could get something to eat and freshen up.

Lizzy walked into the store feeling dazed. She went from aisle to aisle looking for something to eat but she was not feeling hungry. She decided to freshen up instead and as she turned the corner to enter the bathroom, she bumped into a rather handsome guy. He was walking backwards looking at her attentively, as she apologized over and over again. He assured her that it was okay. Lizzy walked into the handicap bathroom to wash up, the line for the lady's room was too long and she didn't want to wait.

Lizzy turned the water on and began to splash water onto her face. She took her top off and started to wash under her arms. She had been sweaty from running and didn't want her only shirt to smell since she didn't bring anything with her. As she bent forward to rinse her body in the sink the door opened. Lizzy was standing there undressed from the waist up, she tried to cup her breast with her hands, but how do you cup size D breasts that stand firmly like trophies on a shelf? It was the guy that she bumped into that walked into the bathroom. He apologized as he stood there staring at her. It seemed as though the words came out in slow motion. Lizzy was shocked with silence. His eyes stared at her breast as they dripped with lathered soap. At first, she wanted him to leave, and then she felt excited. This was as close as she's ever been to a man while standing partly undressed. She felt a rush of heat throughout her entire body. This couldn't be right she thought. Lizzy could barely open her mouth. She softly muttered for him to please leave. He apologized as he walked away. The door shut, and she quickly dried herself off and put her top back on.

Lizzy walked back to the bus and sat down in her seat, her eyes watched as each person entered the bus. Everyone was so different. They talked and dressed so different than anyone she has ever known. Her eyes widened as the guy from the bathroom walked onto the bus. Lizzy's heart started to beat fast, her stomach felt empty, nervous, and excited all at once. Why was she feeling this way?

She didn't even know this person. He wasn't even her type. But then again, she has really never had a type of guy that she was interested in. He stood at least six feet tall, with short spiked blonde hair, the deepest blue eyes and pink full lips. His body looked so strong and his arms so firm. Lizzy took a glance at his backside as he passed by. WOW! she thought his butt is so round. He walked all the way to the back of the bus, but there were no more seats. He walked back up and sat right in front of her. She closed her eyes and took a deep breath as she inhaled the smell of his cologne.

As the bus departed the guy turned to Lizzy and introduced himself as Rick. She shook his hand and looked away. She wanted so bad to have him sit next to her and inhale him the whole ride but the seat next to her was occupied by an older man that smelled of moth balls. Just my luck, Lizzy thought to herself.

Every once in a while, Rick pretended to stretch, as he would turn to look at Lizzy and each time she pretended to be asleep to avoid conversation. On the next stop several people departed and the bus became empty. Lizzy moved to the back of the bus. It was cooler and a much more private. The bus driver played movies towards the front of the bus where most of the people sat and the back was quiet. She prayed that she could admire Rick just a little bit longer. He stepped off the bus with the others and Lizzy felt disappointed thinking he wasn't coming back. The bus driver exited the bus to announce he was leaving. To her surprise, Rick got back on to the bus, he had a drink and a bag in his hand. He walked directly to the back and asked if he could sit with her. She nodded, and he sat. There were no words for some time. Then he asked her where she was from and where she was going. Lizzy answered but kept it short. All she wanted was to feel him close to her, to lay her head on his strong body. To rub her hand against his firm arms and chest. Lizzy didn't want to feel this way, to have these thoughts racing in her head about a stranger, so she closed her eyes and began to fall asleep again.

As the bus went on, it became dark and everyone in the back slept. Without all the voices of the people the movie echoed loudly on the bus. Lizzy slept deep from the excitement of the day. Rick slowly sat up, trying not to wake Lizzy. He stared at her body, imagining her undressed. He wondered why she wore such big clothing if her body was so beautiful, so perfect. Rick slowly stuck his hand under Lizzy's big t-shirt. He began to rub her breast, caressing her nipples until they were hardened. Lizzy was fast asleep still. His penis became hard as he ran his hand to her stomach, into her pants and inside her panties. Lizzy started to feel warm inside, her stomach started to feel as if she was on a roller coaster ride going down fast. Rick rubbed his hand between her legs slowly and softly. Lizzy opened her eyes; he bent forward and kissed her lips softly. It felt so good, this was Lizzy's first time ever being touched by a man or even kissed. Lizzy tremble with every stroke as he caressed her softly round and round. Her body felt hot and wet, as she climaxed.

Rick pushed Lizzy's head down as he pulled himself out of his pants. She didn't know what to do. She looked at him with child like eyes. He whispered to her, "Just take your time." She bent forward and let her mind remember high school stories that her girlfriends shared with her about their adventures. She remembered step by step of how they described their experiences. Lizzy opened her mouth wide and slowly put his penis inside it. She ran her tongue up and down. She could feel his penis become harder. He grabbed her head with one hand and pushed his penis in her mouth with the other, he shot out into her mouth as he moaned softly with pleasure. Lizzy got up and went to the bathroom. She stood looking at herself in the mirror. She had no idea what just happened and still felt like she wanted to do more. She went back to her seat, feeling exhausted Lizzy fell back to sleep, this time in Rick's arms, absorbing the scent of his body and his cologne. In the early morning Lizzy awakened and quietly went to the bathroom to freshen up, without waking Rick. As she brushed her teeth, her mind was racing with thoughts about the way he touched her and how she felt. Then she didn't want to walk out, she felt confused, overwhelmed and ashamed about what happened to her.

Lizzy felt the bus come to a stop while she was in

the bathroom thinking. She was too nervous to walk out, but she knew she had to. She walked out but Rick was gone along with his bags. As the bus drove off in the opposite direction, she looked out the window to see Rick walking. She started to feel anxious, she wanted to tell the bus driver to stop, she bent down and grabbed her purse, she wanted to run and stop him, but it was too late. As she looked down, she saw a paper on the chair. It read, "Thank you for the wonderful time, I'll never forget you, good bye." Lizzy felt this emptiness she had never known before. The bus drove on and that would be the last time she saw Rick. At the next stop, Lizzy sat quietly on the bus eager to get to her destination. She wanted to forget all the feelings that were bottled up inside her. She soon fell asleep feeling depressed, she missed her grandparents.

Morning came, and Lizzy was feeling empty with guilt. She started to remember why she ran away. She wanted so much more, to be able to tell stories of her own, but those weren't the kind of stories she wanted to share, especially not with her own children. The bus made its last stop before it reached her destination. Lizzy went into the store to eat some breakfast. Only two more hours, she kept thinking until she started her life over. She slept the rest of the way, dreaming about all the feelings she felt when Rick touched her, confused.

Chapter two

Lizzy exited the bus after finally reaching her destination. She purchased a map at the bus station, of the city that she decided to call home. She looked over the map carefully. Lizzy asked several people where she should stay for several nights until she found an apartment. Everyone gave her the same advice, they told her to stay away from the strip. Each person explained that the strip was a street where they partied all night, never being able to rest or sleep. Lizzy thought to herself, that's exactly where I want to be right now. She had slept her entire life avoiding life's experiences. So, Lizzy asked her taxi to take her straight to the strip and drop her off at the best hotel. She paid the taxi and walked down the street to what people described as the best hotel. It didn't seem special to her in any way. The area even smelled kind of bad, it had the smell of beer, food, and trash all in one. She priced several different rooms and she decided on a suite that reminded her of home with all the beautiful antique furniture. Lizzy requested the room for a week. The receptionist was a young girl about the same age as Lizzy. She introduced herself as Scarlet. They talked for a while before Lizzy went up to her room. It was nice, Lizzy thought to have found someone so nice and so close to her age to talk to for the week.

Lizzy explained to Scarlet that she was from a very small town and moved suddenly to try something new. Lizzy told her that her parents had passed away and wanted to grow and experience life. Scarlet told her a little about the hot spots in the city and where she could find a good apartment. Lizzy began to feel excited again. Scarlet would be getting off work within the hour and invited Lizzy to hang out with her and some friends. Lizzy agreed to go but told her of her situation with no clothing and how she brought nothing. They decided to go shopping for the night out after Scarlet got off work. Lizzy was nervous, every time she talked to Scarlet, she felt weird inside. Scarlet admired Lizzy's hair and touched it softly. She even admired her body and didn't hide it. She couldn't take her eyes off Lizzy's breast. Lizzy went upstairs to shower and to wait for her new friend to get off work.

Lizzy wanted to shower but realized she didn't bring anything with her, so she called down to the front desk to request several items. She asked that they leave them on the table in the living room. The gentleman at the desk gave her the price and told her that he would be right up. She left the money on the table for the bellman. As Lizzy stood with a towel turning on the shower, she heard someone enter the room. Then, it sounded like they were opening the bathroom door. She yelled and stepped back, it was Scarlet. Scarlet told Lizzy that she got off early and decided to bring up the items herself so that they could talk and get to know each other a little better before shopping. Lizzy was surprised that the girl walked into her bathroom while she was undressed. Lizzy asked her to give her a minute and she would be out. Scarlet walked out of the bathroom but only to get all the things that Lizzy requested. Lizzy told her thank you, but she continued to talk to Lizzy and watch her as she stood there.

Scarlet told Lizzy that she loved both men and women's bodies and really loved how sexy Lizzy's body was. Lizzy was amazed to hear this since no one she knew ever said anything like that to her before. Then, Scarlet started to undress as she entered the shower with Lizzy. Scarlet walked up close and asked Lizzy to relax as she grabbed a wash cloth and started to lather it with body wash. She slowly began to wash Lizzy's back and bent down to her legs from behind. Scarlet slowly ran her tongue down Lizzy, licking her softly. Lizzy jumped forward and told her that she wasn't sure what she was doing.

Scarlet tried to assure Lizzy that it was okay, they would take it slow. She stood up to wash Lizzy's hair as she kissed her slowly. Lizzy's heart was pounding fast now. She was scared but loved everything she was feeling inside. It was a comforting feeling, it was gentle not the same feeling that she felt with Rick. Lizzy felt stimulated, she wondered if this was normal, but didn't care anymore. Scarlet ran her hand over Lizzy's firm breast and whispered to her as she kissed them how she wanted to feel her clit throbbing in her mouth. Scarlet licked Lizzy from her breast, all the way down until she reached between her legs. Lizzy's legs began to tremble, she had never felt this excited and scared before.

Scarlet lowered Lizzy in the tub as the hot water fell onto them. She opened Lizzy's legs and began to run her tongue softly all around her clit. She slowly put her finger in and out of Lizzy, as she sucked her clit like a nipple. Lizzy moaned loudly as she began to feel a tightening feeling in her lower body and then an overwhelming feeling of ecstasy as she climaxed. The girls kissed as they lathered each other's bodies with soap in the warm water. Scarlet then placed Lizzy's hand between her legs and Lizzy began to lather her clit with soap. She kissed Lizzy hard on the mouth passionately, and then lowered herself to Lizzy's breast. She sucked Lizzy's nipples as Lizzy rubbed Scarlet's clit. Lizzy loved the pain she felt with every suck Scarlet took of her nipple. Scarlet and Lizzy moaned loud breathing heavy together, until Scarlet came. Lizzy felt tired as they both dried off. Lizzy felt unsure of what just happened. She felt it wasn't what she wanted but didn't know how to say no.

They both were silent as they dressed. They left together to meet up with Scarlet's friends to shop. Scarlet introduced Lizzy to everyone at a fast food place down the street. Lizzy's body felt drained and hungry. Everyone ate and then walked down the strip to shop. Lizzy's new friend Scarlet begged her to let her put makeup on her and style her hair for the night. Lizzy agreed as long as it was simple. They all went back to Scarlet's friend's apartment and dressed up.

Lizzy had never seen her body the way it looked that night. Her body was so beautiful, with so many curves, her breast were so full and firm. She looked in the mirror and wondered why she never noticed her body before, the way her hips curved into her tiny waist and her dress showed off her backside. Scarlet curled Lizzy's long brown hair and put light makeup on her. She loved outlining her full lips, remembering how it felt to kiss them. Lizzy couldn't believe that she was looking at herself as she stood in front of the mirror. Everyone gathered around Lizzy and helped her pick a dress for their night out.

Lizzy decided to go back to the hotel and rest for a while. As it became dark, she could hear the music playing and the voices of the people's laughter as if it were in her room. Lizzy walked out onto the balcony to see what was going on. She could see the street lined with people dancing, drinking, and eating as they listened to music, several people looked up and admired her. A few minutes later Lizzy's phone rang, and it was Scarlet, she was waiting downstairs. Lizzy looked in the mirror still not believing the image. She felt like she was in a dream, and never wanted it to end.

Lizzy met up with the girls downstairs for her first night out. Scarlet took Lizzy to a club where other friends were waiting. Lizzy's eyes widened as she walked in. To her surprise, it was a club that women exposed their bodies at. This wasn't a club that just anyone was allowed to enter. You could only get in if you were on the VIP list and Lizzy's new friend, Scarlet was. The women on stage were not dressed in any clothing at all.

Lizzy watched every move the girls made. She felt attracted to the women as they danced slowly. She kept thinking all the feelings she had were so wrong. But she just couldn't control them. Lizzy felt hot inside as she watched one of the dancers bend over and down onto the stage, everyone could see her, all of her and the dancers were hot. They looked as if they fell out of magazines. Lizzy told Scarlet that she was feeling excited about being there. Scarlet whispered softly into Lizzy's ear, "The night will only get better." They moved on to another bar where they drank heavily. Lizzy could not control herself and her actions anymore, she drank an over load of liquor. They all walked down the strip to mingle with the crowd. As they walked, Lizzy found it easy to be friendly and flirt with different men as they passed by. She thought to herself, I am having the time of her life! They walked past a big party on the balcony throwing beads down to anyone that lifted their shirts. Lizzy lifted her top, not only did she get all the beads she wanted, the girls put on a show and she was felt up. She felt so high on life that she wanted to take everyone home with her. The girls walked Lizzy back to her room and called it a night, even Scarlet left.

Lizzy wasn't ready to quit yet. She waited until the girls left and walked out on to the balcony on her own. Lizzy danced to the music playing below her and began to undress like she lost in a strip poker game. She pulled her top up and the crowd began to cheer. She bent over towards the crowd and pulled her panties down, so they could see her fully as she slowly pulled her skirt up. The crowd below yelled for more. Lizzy danced provocatively for the crowd. She spotted one guy that she really wanted and welcomed him to come up. He yelled for her to ring him in. She told him to wait at the door and she would come down. Having only her heals on, Lizzy put on a hotel robe and walked down to the first floor to let the man in. She had this eager feeling inside her, something she didn't understand. She could feel the wetness between her legs. She looked at him with desperate eyes standing in front of her and told him to follow her. She walked backwards stumbling and kissing him while drunkenly grabbing his penis. They entered the room, and she walked him out onto the balcony. He asked for alcohol, so Lizzy called down to the receptionist for a bottle of wine. They both sat on the balcony and drank as the crowd partied on into the night. He told her his name was Nathan and that he was just visiting for the weekend.

Lizzy felt out of control, drunken with the large consumption of alcohol in her system and thoughts of someone loving her. She thought as she stared into Nathans eyes that he had to be at least three to four years older, she knew he had to be experienced, but she didn't care. Lizzy felt excited to know that she was in control of this man. She wanted to be desired, touched and kissed all over. She knew what it felt like to lose control and that's what she wanted. She walked over to Nathan and sat on his lap. She faced him with only a robe on. She slowly pulled the strap in the front off and opened her robe so that Nathan could see all of her body as she straddled him. Nathan rubbed his hands all over her first softly and then roughly, this made Lizzy so wet. He walked her into the bedroom and slowly lifted her and laid her onto the bed. She wanted to feel Nathan's touch, his kiss and for him to grind her. Even in her drunken state, she knew she wasn't ready to go all the way. Lizzy knew this wasn't right, but it took her away from all that she felt bad inside about.

Lizzy told Nathan that she wanted to satisfy him in a way that he would never forget. She kissed him softly and ran her tongue down his shoulder to his chest. Nathan's body was fit and so sexy, nothing like she has ever touched or seen before. She caressed his arms as she sat up on him. Lizzy bent forward and ran her tongue on to his nipples, biting and licking them hard. Nathan moaned with both pleasure and pain. She slipped down to his stomach, and kissed him, while stroking her tongue so softly in his belly button. Nathan was ready to burst. She began to lick down to his hard penis, then down to his balls. Lizzy pulled his legs open and sucked between his thighs teasing him as he moaned and begged her to suck him. She ran her tongue up and down his balls as she licked them gently. Nathan turned over and bent forward. She laid her head under Nathan and slowly ran her tongue on to the tip of his penis. Nathan's body begged for her, as he moved with excitement to feel her mouth pleasure him. His penis was hard and throbbing for more. She pulled Nathan down and his penis entered her mouth. He started to thrust uncontrollably into her mouth. She loved the hardness, she wrapped his penis with one hand as he entered her wet mouth. Nathan couldn't control himself anymore, he burst on to her face. Nathan turned to Lizzy and began to rub her between her legs, but Lizzy was too tired to go on. She asked him to call it a night as she walked to the bathroom to clean her face of, then walked him out. Lizzy fell into a deep drunken sleep for the rest of the night. Morning came, and Lizzy felt alone, she wanted to go back home but what would she be going home to? Her grandparents were gone, and she had no one. No one that she cared to be with, that is. Her mother was never there for her, and she wasn't close to anyone in the family, so why go home? Lizzy laid in bed thinking about why she left her comfort behind, why she ran away. She knew it was to find love, true love, to feel loved and yet all she had found was a night of lust and it only made her feel worse.

Lizzy got dressed and left the room to have breakfast. As she sat at the table at the restaurant, she noticed the waiter staring down at her. She ordered and smiled in a flirtatious manner. The waiter came back to the table and she politely asked his name, he responded and told her his name was Carlos. Carlos was tall with the darkest skin, very young and fit. Carlos's skin was dark chocolate and beautiful, so different. She placed an order of fresh fruit, an omelet with tons of bacon and a cup of coffee. Lizzy was starving and so thirsty after a long night of alcohol. She made small talk each time he came to the table, then she asked what time he was done working. Carlos explained to Lizzy that he was only scheduled a four-hour shift, but he had put in some extra hours days prior and was ready to clock out early. He then invited Lizzy to go for a walk in the park with him after her breakfast order was completed and she surprisingly agreed.

Carlos sat with Lizzy at the park and watched her eat. She placed the fresh strawberries into whip cream and slowly bit into it, she moaned softly. "Mmm, the taste of the fresh strawberries are so good." said Lizzy. Carlos was excited as he watched Lizzy eat breakfast, she offered him a bite of her strawberry, and he slowly took a bite as she moved forward and licked the cream from his lips. Lizzy finished eating her entire breakfast and went for a long walk with Carlos, hand in hand. Carlos stood tall and very thin, he was different; she couldn't take her eyes off him. His smile was big, and his eyes were the lightest brown, his head was shaven clean, and his skin was clear. Lizzy really liked Carlos's appearance, he was sharply dressed. He spoke well and was very polite.

Lizzy invited him to shop with her after they ventured into the park. He agreed, and they went from store to store. Lizzy walked into a negligee store and found body oils with flavor. Carlos and Lizzy tasted the oils on each other's skin and decided to buy the cherry flavored oil. The oil was heated and flavored, it was very tasty. They both felt excited with the flavors and the thoughts of the oil. Lizzy could feel the heat rising from her wrist and could imagine the feeling it would have on her clit or around Carlos penis.

Carlos suggested that they walk back to the park. Lizzy agreed, they reached the park with a waterfront. The wind was blowing softly, and the sun was shining down intensely, as Carlos began to kiss Lizzy's lips, he could still taste the oil and felt the heat in his mouth. They could feel the sprinkles of water hitting them from the breeze. It felt good since it was so hot outside. Carlos whispered things in Lizzy's ear that he wanted to do to her. She smiled innocently as the thoughts raced through her mind. He told her that he did not live far from the park and she agreed to venture with him to his residence. Lizzy and Carlos walked about 15 more minutes to his apartment. As they entered Lizzy was surprised to see several people living with him. Carlos had one female, and two male roommates. She was introduced as his *new* friend and everyone received the hint. Everyone left but Darien, he was attracted to Lizzy. He looked at her intensely and tried to make conversation, he talked about his late night but finally got the hint when Carlos interrupted him, and Darien left to his room.

Carlos welcomed Lizzy to sit down and get

comfortable, he asked Lizzy several times nervously if she wanted a drink. Carlos went to the kitchen to grab a glass of wine and Darien came back in. Darien was enticed by the way Lizzys clothes took such form against her body. He began to ask her questions, wanting to know everything about her, especially where she lived before coming to the Party City, Lizzy felt uncomfortable knowing he was being a bit too forward. Carlos came back into the room just in time. Darien excused himself and left the room again. Carlos sat next to Lizzy and began to stroke her hair softly. He leaned forward and softly whispered in her ear saying beautiful things that made her smile. His words took over her mind and she let herself close her eyes and listen to them as he spoke of the things he wanted to do to her.

Lizzy turned to Carlos and put her hands against his face as she pulled him to her slowly and kissed his lips. They looked deep into each other's eyes and breathed heavily into one another. Lizzy took off Carlos's shirt and opened the oil and let it drop down his chest as she licked it down to his belt. She stopped and opened his pants looking deep into his eyes with pure ecstasy. Her eyes had a longing for him that made him hard. She unzipped his pants as he laid back and she poured oil onto his hard penis. Carlos couldn't help himself anymore just the feeling of the heat and knowing she would soon have her mouth wrapped around him made him want to be inside her. Carlos grabbed her head and held it tightly as he pushed his penis slowly to her mouth. She licked him as she let him slowly enter her mouth. Lizzy wanted to give him so much more but knew she wasn't ready. He came deep in her mouth.

Carlos and Lizzy were surprised to see Darien standing and watching. Darien asked Lizzy if he could join them, she looked towards Carlos for approval and he agreed. Darien pulled Lizzy's dress up and began rubbing her clit, as she kissed Carlos then Darien undressed Lizzy. Carlos and Darien took turns licking her clit and breast as Lizzy moaned and begged for more. Lizzy felt so much pain but pleasure as Darien fingered her. She begged for more, until she was dripping with cum. Darien and Carlos were so excited, they wanted more. Lizzy started to have thoughts of how she was going to tell them that she was still a Virgin. She quickly stood up and began to dress. She grabbed her bags and walked to the door. She opened the door and started to walk out as Darien and Carlos sat up trying to get dressed, confused. She thought in her mind that she had to find the right man, someone that loved her and wasn't using her for simple pleasures. Carlos ran down after Lizzy. She was honest and told him she had never been with a man before. She said she had never been loved, she longed and desired that and didn't want to have this emptiness he offered her. Carlos apologized not realizing Lizzy was a Virgin still and not experienced. Lizzy walked off alone, and Carlos let her.

Lizzy went back to her hotel room and slept for the rest of the day. She heard a knock on the door, it was Scarlet. She told Scarlet about her day with Carlos and Darien. Scarlet thought it was a wonderful experience, but she was concerned about her being a Virgin in the Party City. Scarlet assured her not to worry, she wouldn't be for much longer. They laid together, talking all through the night as they touched and kissed each other. Lizzy wasn't sure if this was what she wanted for herself. She knew she wanted change and she knew she wanted to find herself but is this all that she was worth or is this all that she had become? Did she really turn into her mother? Scarlet went down stairs to work and Lizzy spent the rest of the day laying in bed thinking.

Soon it was dark, and the music began to play. Lizzy felt and itch to go out and drink, to explore and meet Mr. Right. She had decided to find the right man that was going to deflower her. She stood out on the balcony watching and thinking, so restless. Why had she run away? Was it to be in love or to be reckless and hurt herself more? Lizzy thought that she was becoming more and more destructive and couldn't live this way. The alcohol always brought out both the best and worst in her. Lizzy got dressed and decided to venture out on her own. She walked for some time until she found a club that was packed with people dancing. She drank well into the night. The dance floor had cages on all four corners and the music was very loud. Lizzy walked up to one of the cages, and the people pulled her up. As she danced with them she closed her eyes, feeling the music deep within her. The pounding of the speakers, the beat was so loud and intense. The alcohol was taking its full affect. When she walked into the club she did not realize it was a gay club. She felt free dancing to the loud beats. Everyone was dancing so close and rubbing each other's bodies together. She felt hands all over her, touching her, grinding against her.

Oh, how she wanted to undress, to be free and feel all those bodies against hers. Everyone was dancing so fast jumping up and down to the beat, touching, and kissing. Lizzy kissed everyone in the cage allowing their hands all over her. She could feel the beat rushing through her body dancing faster, kissing harder, touching bodies. They rubbed her so hard and so fast that she came all over herself in the cage. Lizzy was amazed at the way she was behaving. How easy it was to be pleased and to have no connections. She felt on top of the world, so empowered by the sensual feeling of it all and so worthless at the same time, intoxicated and confused.

Lizzy climbed down as the people in the cage continued to dance and party. She went to the bar to get a drink. She stood there, attracted to the bartender. What a beautiful sight! The woman was not very young at all, but very sexy in her drunk eyes. Lizzy wanted to get back home, to rest after her intense night. The bartender introduced herself as Suzy and asked her to wait so that she could sober up before leaving. Lizzy sat and drank water until the club closed. Suzy talked Lizzy into letting her walk her home. They talked and walked for about two blocks. Lizzy invited her up, Suzy declined. Lizzy was confused, she didn't understand why this person wouldn't want her, why she didn't jump at the chance to be with her. This was the first time Lizzy was feeling rejection.

Lizzy walked upstairs alone. She went into the bathroom and ran the water in the tub. She felt the same way she did the day she ran away. She wanted to run away again and never looking back, who had she become? Was this all she would ever be, a one-night experience and feeling alone? Yes, everyone wanted her but for how long? She finished up in the shower and went to bed praying for a better day.

Chapter three

Lizzy woke up late in the afternoon hungry, feeling better now that her buzz had subsided. She decided to get the newspaper and look for a job. It would be something that would keep her busy and keep her mind off partying so much. Lizzy went downstairs, sat in the restaurant, and read the job advertisements. She circled a few and made some phone calls. After having breakfast, she wanted to take a long walk, get some fresh air, and think. She went back upstairs grabbed a throw blanket, a bag with a book and walked out the door. She ventured off towards the park, stopped at the corner store and then purchased snacks and a drink. After arriving at the park, she laid down her blanket and read for a little while. Then, she sat up and snacked as she watched all the couples and felt bad inside that she wasn't anything better than her mother. Lizzy thought long about what she could do to change her way of thinking, but her mind kept going back to the way intimacy made her feel. It had been an empowering experience for her, but she wanted that with someone that loved her.

While Lizzy was sitting admiring all the happy couples, she received a call from a small book store owner. He was returning her call from the message she left at breakfast about a job he posted. Lizzy made arrangements for an interview the next day. She was excited and wanted to share her great news with someone but whom? She had no one to talk to really. Lizzy packed her stuff and started off back home. She thought as she walked home how she wanted to find a wonderful man. Someone that she could spend the rest of her life with, someone that made her feel all those wonderful feelings of ecstasy but someone she could share so much more with too. Could she find that in this big city or should she go back home, she thought. Tomorrow couldn't come soon enough, she couldn't wait for her interview at the book store.

Early in the morning Lizzy walked to her job interview smiling as she felt better about the day. She hoped that the interview would go well and prayed that she would get the job. She felt nervous as she walked the longest four blocks, thinking about not having any kind of experience. There was a breeze and it started to rain as she hurried through the streets. She was still feeling a little restless, but she had something new that held her mind. The thought of meeting new people made her feel great inside because it would be the right way, through a job.

She walked into the bookstore and it smelled like fresh coffee. It was a professional environment with lots of well established business men and women. The book store was in the back of the coffee shop. Lizzy let the cashier know she was there for an interview and ordered a coffee as she sat patiently and waited. The owner of *More than just a book*, came out. Lizzy saw the owner, he was very old but very handsome.

She thought that he was dressed very sharp and smelled nice. Mr. Lovinger explained to Lizzy that his wife had grown sick and had was unable to work anymore. He explained that his wife had a brain tumor.

Lizzy felt torn about the story but just wanted to hear that she was hired already. Mr. Lovinger told Lizzy she would oversee the store since he couldn't be there as much anymore. She smiled and thanked him several times. That day went fast with all the training she had to go through. She learned a lot and was very surprised that Mr. Lovinger was allowing her to take over and open the store alone the next day, along with the cashiers. There were four cashiers, two for the coffee shop and two for the book store. Each employee had a different shift and Lizzy was happy that she was scheduled all day.

Lizzy couldn't wait to get back to the hotel to tell Scarlet. She was glowing with enthusiasm. She walked into the hotel and walked up to the front desk tell Scarlet the great news and as always it was a call for a celebration. They agreed to meet up at an outdoor restaurant for dinner and drinks. Scarlet invited several other friends while Lizzy changed into something much more comfortable. They took a taxi to the restaurant. The crowd was great, so many new faces, she thought. Very elegant place, this would be her first time with this group of people. She was from a little town and didn't know anything about fine dining or the flavors of wine. She sat there and let the moment capture her as the cool breeze hit her. The sweet smell of leathery cologne, the taste of the wine, the soft jazz playing in the background and the attractive man sitting next to her made the night perfect.

James was such a classy man, and Lizzy kept thinking how wonderful it would be to feel his soft lips on hers and to be able to stare into his sexy hazel eyes. She knew that he was attracted to her as well by the way he smiled at her. She talked the night away feeling slightly buzzed and saying a little too much at times but in this crowd, no one judged her, everyone was so nice and welcoming. The night ended, and she wanted so badly for James to ask her to go home with him. She wanted him to take full advantage of her, to grab her tightly and kiss her. But he was being such a gentleman and only smiled from a distance. That turned her on more. They stayed until the restaurant closed and as she walked towards the street to call for a taxi home, James followed behind her to make sure she was safe while waiting. She turned to James and thought, why do you have to be so great? James reached for her hand, pulled her to him and kissed her passionately. His lips were just as she imagined, so soft. His cologne was very manly, and he smelled of money. He waved down a taxi and they got in together. No words were exchanged, only glances back and forth as her mind raced with lustful thoughts. They arrived at the hotel and James walked her to her room. She asked him to come in and he did. She expected more, wanted so much more from him but he was disciplined, he was different, not at all what she expected and wanted.

James called down for wine, and Lizzy freshened up in the bathroom. They sat outside on the balcony and stared at each other. James stood up and grabbed Lizzy by the hand, with no words he walked her into the bedroom, and slowly undressed her from head to toe as he kissed her softly. Lizzy felt so turned on. She was scared, knowing this man was much older and very experience. She kept thinking how she would tell him that she was still a virgin and not ready for sex.

There wasn't time for words. This was it, this was the man she would share this experience with. James dimmed the light in the bedroom by shutting off the lamps and leaving the bathroom door cracked. He turned on some music from the clock radio on the side of the bed and slowly pulled Lizzy close to him. She was so wet with the thought of what was to come. He touched her body softly and kissed her breast as he slipped his hand between her legs. She lay back on the bed and opened her legs for him to see all of her. He slipped his tongue down her inner thigh, teasing her by getting close but never completely tasting her. He watched Lizzy as she touched herself wanting him so bad. She ran her fingers gently on her clit, wanting him to take over. James was in full control of her body now as she longed to feel him. James bent down again and finally ran his tongue over her clit. She trembled wanting more, but he only teased her with strokes of his tongue then he would watch her as she pleased herself. James could see that she was wet and finished by licking her until she came in his mouth, dripping with excitement of the wonderful feeling of his tongue and lips caressing her clit.

Lizzy got up and started to unbutton James pants. All she could think about was pleasing him in return, but he stopped her. He told her he had to get home. Lizzy felt unsure of what just happened. She thought, was it okay to not please a man and only let him please her and shouldn't this lust be shared? He kissed her gently on the lips and walked out the door. Lizzy's mind always took her away, she thought about how she looked while lying in bed, with her legs wide open. She wanted to know what James thought of her body, and if he was as excited as she was. She started to feel as though maybe he didn't get excited about her body and possibly she wasn't sexy enough for him. She let her mind run wild with so many thoughts until she fell fast asleep.

The next day came and went, nothing exciting at the coffee shop, just a lot of paperwork, and the same old faces came in and out throughout the day. Lizzy longed for romance, for passion, to fall in love and explore her life with one man. Lizzy was getting ready to leave the store when she picked up an invitation from under the door. It was an event. This big city always had such great events, but she didn't know anyone and didn't want to go alone. The crowd that she had been spending time with wasn't into all that business stuff, just partying and socializing. Lizzy's job took her to another place, with different people.

The next day, while Lizzy was opening the store, someone tapped her on the shoulder. It was an older guy, he introduced himself as Cris. It is nice to meet you Cris, Lizzy responded. Cris, explained that he was the one that left the flyer under the store door after closing and wasn't sure if she received it. Lizzy told him that she had received the flyer when she left the store late last night.

Cris asked Lizzy if she would like to attend the event with him and she gladly accepted. Cris agreed to meet Lizzy at the store to pick her up and introduce her to everyone. Lizzy worked until 5:00 pm that day. She was super excited about the possibilities of meeting someone there. A man that had everything going for him, someone that she could share her life with. Lizzy closed her eyes as she sat in the break room. She started to remember the home she left behind, all her friends and comfort. What had she become? Could she ever go back to that small town and be that small-town girl? No, Lizzy thought as she jumped up and ventured to the bathroom. Looking in the mirror Lizzy thought of how beautiful her body took shape in her dress. She wondered again if she would meet that someone special.

Lizzy met Cris at the store, he was so happy to see her. They took a taxi to the event and chatted on the way over. Cris introduced her to all the business people there and Lizzy mentioned to everyone about all the great specials they were having this up coming week at the book store. She felt good inside knowing she was doing something positive for Mr. Lovinger and his wife. As she turned to shake another hand, she noticed him. By glance but couldn't take him off her mind. He stood tall, very confident, and so handsome. His smile brightened the entire room. Lizzy avoided making contact with this unknown man. She couldn't stop looking at him from a distance. Why hadn't he noticed her? He was so busy talking and doing business that he hadn't even glanced her way. She watched him, thinking of how she just wanted him to look at her.

Lizzy wanted to leave but not before she introduced herself to the handsome man. She made sure she walked towards his path. Still nothing, he made no effort, didn't acknowledge her at all. Finally, she sat down with a group of people that were enjoying the night with laughter and wine. There he was, his smile so sexy, he turned to her and finally he noticed. Oh, did he notice. Lizzy was excited, he sat next to her and started to talk. Lizzy was so nervous, she turned away not really acknowledging his words, just thinking about what she wanted from him. He introduced himself as Marcos. Lizzy's eyes looked straight at him as he looked deeply into her. She felt so nervous, as if he undressed her without even touching her. His stare was deep, and she could feel him burning through her. Lizzy wanted him to get close enough to whisper words of longing in her ear and to take her in his arms and passionately kiss her. Lizzy wanted more, she wanted to tell him to meet her, to go home with her. But, was this the right environment? How could she do it, plus Cris was right by her side. Was she being obvious, so obvious that everyone could see how she wanted him? Lizzy stood up and decided to end the night, she told everyone bye as she walked out. Marcos walked towards her and handed her his business card. Lizzy knew this wouldn't be the night, but it wasn't over either. She would make sure he knew she wanted him. She took a taxi home and sat quietly thinking about still wanting to go home to the country. Why wasn't she confident enough to talk to him more? Why had she waited all night?

Lizzy started to think how James didn't want her to please him and that made her feel unsure of herself. What had she done wrong? Was all the excitement gone? Had she lost her sensuality? No, no that wasn't it at all. She made sure as soon as she got home to leave Marcos a message. She wanted to learn more about him, so she invited him over to the store for coffee.

Marcos never responded, and Lizzy started to lose concentration at work just thinking about him. Could he be the one? Lizzy thought about why it meant so much for her to meet him again, to spend time with him, to talk to him. She wanted more than that but how could she express it without being so forward? The day was coming to an end and Lizzy was feeling worn from her thoughts. She was turning off all the lights and making sure everything was in order when there was a knock at the stores locked door.

Yes! It was him, it was Marcos! How she felt so enticed, so many things racing through her head. She wanted to run into his arms and kiss him so hard. She had to calm down, her heart raced with lust. Lizzy walked to the door, she smiled seductively. She couldn't hide it, she wanted him. She opened the door and told him that the store was closed as if to invite him somewhere else, possibly straight into her arms. Marcos apologized saying that he worked all day and had been too busy to respond.

Lizzy invited Marcos in and walked him to the back of the store. She had to make a quick call. Lizzy called Mr. Lovinger and explained that she would be staying at the store an hour later. He didn't mind at all, she said she wanted to tidy the store up a bit. Lizzy went back to Marcos and asked him if he wanted to stay and chat for a bit. He smiled right into her and said that he would love to. Marcos came prepared with a bottle of wine in his business brief case, how convenient she thought. They both looked at each other almost as if for the first time. Lizzy walked to the front of the store to get two glasses from the coffee shop area. She was taken back by the name of the wine but thought how clever. Ménage A Trios, "I've never had that before" Lizzy said to Marcos, "Is it good?" Marcos turned to her and looked at her lips as he said, "It's very tasty." The room became hot, they could feel each other's desire. They each knew they wanted one another, so badly. Lizzy fanned herself with her hand, as Marcos poured the wine. Lizzy took a sip, it went down so smoothly, the smell of it was very welcoming and the man in front of her was all she wanted to end the night with. Marcos served both him and Lizzy another glass of wine and sat down. He explained that he was exhausted from the day and wanted to know how her day went. Lizzy thought this is completely different, why isn't he kissing me? Why isn't he reacting to the way I want him? He continued to talk about the hustle and bustle of the corporate world. Lizzy had no idea what he was talking about since she was never exposed to that before. She reached out to ask Marcos a question and placed her hand over his, he smiled and slowly leaned forward to kiss her. She wanted it so bad, she had waited patiently for that one kiss. Marcos was very passionate, he stood up and held her close to him, talked to her and said all the right things, all the things she needed to hear.

Marcos invited her home with him, Lizzy thought, finally! I can't wait! Yet, she responded respectfully and said that she would love to. They drove to his home. Lizzy absolutely loved the area, she wanted to get a place of her own and thought it would be great to live nearby. They walked into his home together and Marcos showed her around, he made her feel completely comfortable.

Lizzy was taken back by his expensive taste, it was

so manly and yet so sophisticated. Everything she expected it to be and more. He poured her a glass of wine and offered her something to eat. Lizzy was starving but declined, all she wanted was to fall into his arms. Lizzy asked Marcos if she could freshen up and he walked her into his bathroom and showed her around. His closet was lined perfectly with his clothes, each color coordinated, from casual to work suites. His shoes were lined in shelves, ties in order. Her eyes were widened by the way Marcos lived.

Marcos handed Lizzy a towel and started the shower for her. Marcos walked out leaving the door cracked, he watched Lizzy undress. Lizzy didn't pay attention and didn't realize she was being watched. She slowly undressed, first taking off her top, then her bra. Marcos started to get erect as he watched Lizzy remove her skirt, then slowly slipping off her panties. As he watched Lizzy's panties drop to the floor, he became really turned on. He started to touch himself as he stood and watched her. She stood there with only her heals on fully undressed. Then, Lizzy slowly slipped off her heals and walked to the shower. She entered and shut the glass door behind her. Marcos watched as the water hit her face, dripping down her body, rolling off the arch of her back. Her wet body was very sexy to Marcos. Lizzy started to lather her breast, then bending over to reach her legs. Marcos was really excited now as he saw her soapy wet pussy, he started to work himself fast. Marcos walked towards the bathroom and opened the door, undressed with his penis fully erect. Lizzy was so excited to see him enter the shower. She watched as he walked in and shut the door. Lizzy felt lustful remembering her experience with Scarlet, thinking it would be the same way. It didn't cross her mind that he would want to stick his hard penis in her.

Marcos stood behind Lizzy and kissed her back softly, holding her tightly from behind. Lizzy felt so comfortable with Marcos, she wanted this, and she longed for him to want her in return. Lizzy turned her head towards him and licked his lips as the warm water fell over them. She was wet now, pulsating between her legs longing for Marcos to touch her. He pushed Lizzy forward as he rubbed himself between her legs. Lizzy kept thinking she was ready for this but something in her said, no, not now. She grabbed his penis with her hand, she felt how big he was, how hard he felt and turned to him and kissed him passionately. His lips and tongue so soft, with the water dripping from them. She moved her hand up and down on his hard penis. Marcos pushed her head down softly and she licked him from his chest all the way down to pleasure him, she placed him in her mouth. He slowly moved in and out of Lizzy's mouth as he watched her look up at him. Marcos was so excited that he could no longer hold back. He moaned with pleasure, as he came, and she let it drip down the sides of her mouth. Lizzy was pleased with herself that she made him cum so hard. She stood up and rinsed her mouth with the shower water.

Lizzy knew she was not ready to give herself to a

man like this. How could she be so wrong about this? How could she fall for this man by merely being attracted to him, how did she get to this place? Marcos walked out of the shower handing Lizzy a towel, she couldn't look at him. Lizzy grabbed her clothes and walked out of the bathroom. Her mind was racing again, she felt scared inside, thinking she needed to leave. Marcos was a gentleman, he walked out of the bathroom and shut the door, so she could get dressed. Lizzy pulled her hair back and dressed quickly. She walked out into the living room and looked at Marcos, she walked into his arms and felt calm again. Marcos embraced her in a reassuring way. He walked her to the couch, and she sat. He walked to the kitchen and poured her another glass of wine.

Lizzy felt relaxed as they sat face to face, talking, passing kisses every once in a while, in between conversation. Lizzy was taken aback by his intelligence. Marcos allowed Lizzy to tell him her story, where she was from and how she got to the Party city.

She talked for hours wanting to share her story. Then, Marcos made it a point to tell Lizzy that he needed to wake early and called a taxi for her to leave. That's when Lizzy felt overwhelmed with feelings of emptiness and pain. She didn't think he would ask her to leave so soon. Why couldn't she stay and leave in the morning? What had she done so wrong? Did she say too much, too soon? Feelings of confusion filled her mind, but she smiled and thanked him for a wonderful night. Lizzy walked out the door and entered the taxi. Was this all that he wanted? Is this what getting to know her meant? She left feeling alone, wanting to go home back to the little town that always allowed her to feel safe and fall apart. Lizzy started to realize that she was doing it all the wrong way. Searching for a fantasy, something that was real to the touch, to the act of but not to the heart. This entire time she was accepting the things that everyone wanted from her but not demanding what she wanted in return. How could she be so clueless to this thing called love? Why hadn't anyone ever taught her the right way? She thought how it was perfect for her grandparents, but how her mother did it all wrong. Why was she so torn between love and lust?

Lizzy went up to her room, she wanted to call home. To call Bill and ask how things were going with the house and land. To cry, to reach out to all the wonderful things she knew and grew fond of as a child. But she couldn't. How could she call Bill and sound okay? He would know right away that something was wrong, and she didn't want that. Lizzy couldn't tell him what she turned into, what she had put herself through. She sat for a while longer trying to calm down. Lizzy decided that she couldn't sit at home and sulk any longer. She dressed and walked down to the lobby. Scarlet had already walked out for the night. Lizzy didn't want to be alone. She didn't feel like doing the same things she did before. Lizzy felt torn inside, what had she learned or accomplished this whole time?

What was she really doing? Had she begun to punish herself for all the things her mother was and her grandmother wasn't?

Lizzy walked out of the Hotel and walked down the street, not feeling anything at all, not knowing what she wanted. While walking Lizzy ran right into the Theater and decided to watch a show alone, since she wouldn't be good company anyhow. She felt excited about watching a live, romantic performance. She had never experienced anything like this before. She walked in and sat at a table in front of the stage, she ordered a drink and felt relaxed again. Lizzy watched the couples walk in dressed up, hand in hand. She wondered if she would ever have that. She talked herself out of feeling bad again and held her smile.

The show began, and the lights dimmed low. She had a candle gleaming on her table and her mind raced with thoughts of Marcos. She tried to focus on the show but could only think about the way she felt inside. Lizzy was confused about how she was feeling, about how things were left. She kept thinking how her heart was so heavy about someone she just met, someone so wonderful and yet so toxic for her. She sat quietly and was slowly drawn into the show. It was so romantic and passionate, just what Lizzy needed and wanted. As she sat watching the show an older, very attractive man walked up and asked if he could join her. He explained that all the seats were taken, and he was running late from the office. Lizzy smiled and said it was fine. The man introduced himself as Michael. He had a beautiful smile, very welcoming. Lizzy sat quietly and became absorbed into the performance. The show had so many things in it that Lizzy could relate to. She started to feel happy again, almost forgetting about her last experience. Michael looked into Lizzy with his green eyes as the candle gleamed between them. He offered her a drink, Lizzy accepted. How could she say no to this attractive man? He was so handsome, or was it the alcohol she had been drinking with Marcos? Michael ordered her a mixed drink, something she had never had before. An unusual name to her, he ordered her a Pina Colada Cocktail. What a unique name for a drink, so very naughty as well. Just right for the moment, it brought laughter after he said it, she loved the way it rolled out of his mouth.

"So, Lizzy, how do you like the taste of a cocktail?" Michael asked. Lizzy's response was "it's very smooth." The name and creamy texture of the drink came into play with the mood and the moment. Lizzy felt very good after her first drink, but very intoxicated. Michael's cologne was so welcoming to Lizzy. She loved the smell of it, but it reminded her of Rick's cologne. Lizzy started to feel light headed and very overwhelmed with emotions from the experiences she had since she left home. She wanted to enjoy this wonderful man sitting in front of her, but she didn't want to scare him off with her stories like she did with Marcos, or so she thought that's what happened. Lizzy wanted to call it a night. But Michael didn't let her, he sensed she needed the company and asked her to share some time with him.

Chapter Four

Lizzy walked with Michael but didn't say much. Her mind raced with memories and disappointments. Michael started to feel like he did something wrong, as if she didn't want him by her side. He thought maybe he should leave her alone since they really didn't know each other. Michael asked Lizzy if she wanted him to leave, but Lizzy responded by saying no and she apologized, explaining it was a long day and had nothing to do with him. Michael smiled and rubbed her back in reassurance, she knew she did the right thing by allowing herself to enjoy and get to know him.

Michael and Lizzy came to an outdoor restaurant where live music was playing. Lizzy needed something to sober her up, so Michael ordered her fried calamari. He explained that the breaded batter would help her absorb some of the alcohol in her system. Lizzy smiled at the way Michael quickly took the role of nurturing her. She was impressed and grateful. Maybe there was hope for her still. Just maybe God was giving her a sign that she still had to keep her hopes up for that wonderful man.

They sat listening to the music, in silence at first looking at each other from across the table. Michael talked a little bit about himself but not really revealing too much. Lizzy started to sober up and converse with Michael about her new job. Michael was surprised to find out Lizzy was working at the, More Than just a Book Store. Michael loved that place and was pleased to know he could see her more since he frequently had coffee there.

Lizzy was surprised but happy that he wanted to learn more about her. Michael was very uplifting and positive. As the night went on Lizzy became relaxed but very tired. The day had been very draining for her. Lizzy asked Michael to walk her home, and he gladly accepted. Michael and Lizzy walked together, gazing into each other, talking, and laughing on the walk home. Lizzy was feeling much better, and almost entirely forgot about Marcos. Michael walked with Lizzy into the hotel and to her door. He thanked Lizzy for sharing the night with him and said he couldn't wait to see her again. He waved and walked off, Lizzy was glowing. She kept thinking how wonderful it felt to have a normal date. She walked into her room and fell backwards on to her bed. "Oh, how wonderful you are Michael!" Lizzy whispered. She kept thinking about how nice the night ended. Lizzy started to undress and noticed the red blinking light on the phone. She called down to the lobby and they informed her that there was a message from a man named Marcos for her. Lizzy ran down and picked up the note.

"Dear Lizzy, I could not sleep thinking about you, your beautiful body, with so many curves, the way your lips tasted and the look in your eyes as you had me in your mouth. I wanted to see you again, but you had already left by the time I arrived." Lizzy's heart was pounding hard now. She wanted Marcos in her life so bad. This was more than she could handle for a day. Michael was amazing, she thought to herself.

Lizzy was lying in bed restless now. Thinking to herself why she continued to torment herself with all the emptiness, the unknown, the lust, the longing to feel whole and making all the wrong choices. Why did she want Marcos so bad? It was all wrong and Lizzy knew it, she knew it was lust and nothing more. Her attraction for Marcos consumed everything in her. She picked up the phone to call Marcos but knew it was too late. She couldn't call him now, he had to work the next day. Then there was a knock at her door, she rushed over to open it, thinking Marcos came back but it was Michael. He told Lizzy that he did not want to be alone. Lizzy welcomed him into her room smiling compassionately. She really didn't feel like company, her mind was heavy with Marcos on it, but how could she turn this man away. He had taken her from desperation to feeling like she was worth something again. Lizzy asked Michael to stay the night, she asked him if he wanted a drink, but Michael said that he only wanted to share her company.

So, Lizzy and Michael lay side by side holding each other, nothing more. She closed her eyes and felt the comfort of his arms wrapped around her. The smell of his cologne from his arm under her nose. How enticing it was and yet no desire for anything more than to be held. Slowly she started to doze off, while having a warm and safe feeling inside. She finally closed her eyes, falling into a deep sleep. Michael slept comfortably with Lizzy, and then her alarm went off for work. Lizzy jumped thinking it was all a dream. But Michael was still there lying in bed with her. It was well into the afternoon and she had to be at work in two hours. Lizzy wanted to call in and sleep with this wonderful man for the rest of the day. But she knew Marcos would be awaiting her arrival at work. She just knew it by the letter he left her, the time he took to bring it to her, the wonderful & lustful feelings he had for her. Lizzy laid her head back down and held onto Michael as her mind raced. Lizzy was caught in this love triangle, having feelings for two wonderful men. Could this be happening to her? Well it was, and it didn't feel good at all. It made her feel even more unsure of who she had become. Why was she so much like her mom? Did her mom have a story that was untold, something that hurt her so bad that she was unable to love? She lay quietly as she felt this inner pain of how she completely cut her mom off.

Lizzy didn't understand why she had judged her mom so harshly, and now had a better understanding of why her grandparents always embraced her mom and loved her just the same. What had they known that she didn't know? She felt torn and ashamed inside for her actions, for not loving her mom, for sharing herself for all the wrong reasons. Lizzy wanted to feel loved so bad, to feel wanted but she kept giving herself for the sake of a small fix. Lizzy was learning that this was a cruel world and she was contributing to it by hurting herself and sharing herself in all the wrong ways.

This was not a solution but rather, her quick fix to feeling better for that moment. They said all the right things, shared their time with her, even spent money on her when she didn't need all that. It felt great for the moment, for the time it was taking place but really it wasn't what she wanted. Why had she been so afraid all this time to love? Why had she fallen out of love with herself, or was it that she never knew what true love was? There was no other reason that she couldn't find love but that she had no love for herself. There was no time to reflect on that right now, she had to get to work and figure out what she was going to do with the men in her life.

Lizzy and Michael got up. She showered and walked with him downstairs to have a late breakfast after he freshened up. She thanked him for a peaceful night and walked to work. Lizzy waited all day for Marcos to come, but he never did. She couldn't concentrate on anything. Her mind was full of wishful thoughts and unanswered questions once again. She closed the store and neither Michael nor Marcos came. She walked home, thinking as the breeze hit her face. She walked to a bar and sat alone, still with her mind full of thoughts. Had she been so horrible to love? Is that why her mother walked away from her so early on? Is that where all this emptiness had come from? Lizzy started to remember the mean words her mother used towards her when she was young. She remembered why her grandparents took her away from her mom. Could that be where this emptiness comes from, the need to run away and the desire to be loved so badly? But what caused her mom to be so abusive to her? Was it because she had also been abused, did her mom have hate in her heart from not knowing her dad? Too much to think about, Lizzy thought it's time to have a blast and forget about all the pain.

Lizzy sat at the bar and ordered a shot of buttery nipple. The taste was so rich and made her feel so much better. The music was from a juke box and played softly as she drank down a couple of beers. She watched the people around her, wondering how many other people were drinking from emptiness.

A group of college kids her age walked in and sat at a table, drinking, and having a blast. The group talked and laughed of the good old days. Lizzy missed home more but refused to let the night get the best of her. She was taking charge of her night and she was determined to have a blast. Lizzy paid for her last drink and walked out. This crowd was going too slow for her. Lizzy walked down the strip and looked for the closest place to dance and let the music consume her. She walked into a club where the music was loud, the crowd was wild, and everyone was dancing. This is really what she missed and needed to make it right. Lizzy ordered a drink and then another, she was forgetting about everything right now. She walked on to the dance floor and began to dance alone, to feel the music, to long for someone to take her home, she felt alone.

Lizzy wanted that fix, that quick fix. She longed for all the wrong things in her mind.

She danced and found herself attracted to someone across the dance floor sitting at the bar. Lizzy slowly danced towards him. She watched him as he stood up and walked to her. He looked young, about her age. He stood tall, shoulders broad, dark thick hair, beautiful brown eyes. He smiled as she danced and made her way to him. Lizzy walked off the dance floor and tumbled a bit towards him feeling the buzz. He was so handsome she thought in her mind as she felt the effects of the alcohol and the weight of the day on her shoulders. She smiled and introduced herself as Lizzy, he smiled and said, "I'm pleased to meet you, my name is Alexander." He had this amazing accent that made her giggle a little.

Lizzy sat at the bar and Alexander sat down with her, the more he talked the more humor she found in him. The laughter was unexpected since she had so many downfalls, so many setbacks, so many heartaches but she felt okay inside enough to share laughter. Lizzy knew that no matter what she endured or what happened to her she was strong enough to deal with all the things that came at her. Lizzy smiled at this man in front of her and talked the night away, every once in a while, really looking into him, seeing his beauty, and all the innocents he carried in him. The way he talked about normal things for his age. He didn't seem to care about finding love or anything to that extreme.

He said he was waiting for love to find him, for love to take form in front of him and nothing more, Alexander explained. He told Lizzy that in life we cannot predict the future, nor can we determine who is best for us. He told Lizzy to stop chasing something that she was never going to find while on a path to destruction. Lizzy agreed and for the first-time things started to make sense. She was very intrigued by Alexander's words, by the things he had knowledge of and yet all she wanted to do was embrace him, for him to take her in his arms and hold her.

To feel him close to her, to taste his lips. He was so strong, so well kept, so smart about all the thing she knew nothing about. Lizzy invited Alexander home, but he declined because he was with friends. Lizzy started to let her mind take her away. She started to feel that empty feeling again but not for long. She corrected her inner emotions. She no longer allowed her emotions to take a hold of her. She talked herself into feeling great inside! Lizzy left and walked down to her hotel. The minute she walked into the door to her room she picked up the phone and longed to call her mom, to call Bill, but it was already so late. Lizzy called downstairs and ordered some food. She sat for a moment and thought about all the healing she needed. Lizzy realized why she looked for love in literally all the wrong places and people.

Intimacy and lust felt great, but it was short term. She started to understand where she was doing it all wrong. Lizzy decided to make amends with her mom and heal her heart. Then she thought possibly she would learn to understand what real love is and not some magic for the time being lust. Early in the morning Lizzy called her mom and decided to go home to meet her, to talk and to really get to know her. Lizzy scheduled a flight home, she thought about all the exciting events in her life that took place. All the wonderful experiences and the wisdom she grew from each and every event. But wanted to heal internally, to experience true love that she so desired. The love that her grandparents taught her, the love she deserved. Not the way it felt to be used, controlled or for the time being lust.

Lizzy went downstairs and told Scarlet she was leaving home. Scarlet was sad but understood and wished her well. Lizzy and Scarlet shopped for luggage, held hands like old friends and enjoyed the entire day. Scarlet helped Lizzy pack. Lizzy thanked Scarlet for embracing her and helping her while she was there. Lizzy walked out of the hotel, never looking back. Walking straight into the taxi, through the drive towards the airport having no regrets of her choices just looking forward to getting home and meeting up with her mom, all her friends and spending time in the comfort of who she had become and letting go of who she had been all these years.

Lizzy arrived in her little town and her mom picked her up from the airport. There was silence the entire ride. Lizzy's mom knew she was different, she could feel the maturity in her and sensed the change. They walked into the house and Lizzy's friends were there to greet her. Lizzy felt at peace, she walked upstairs to put her luggage in her room and realized she belonged there. There was no other place than home that she needed to be to complete this journey in healing. Everyone agreed to sit outside like old times, they walked towards that old oak tree in the back of the property, Lizzy sat there in silence as everyone talked, remembering the nightmare, thankful it was far behind her. She was happy to know her mom was home, cooking in the kitchen while she was out back sitting on the chairs, feet up on a crate. She laughed the night away with innocence, her heart full of love and comfort.

Lizzy felt free of her inner emptiness, she understood now that it was up to her to let go and move forward. To forgive her mom, to love herself, to decide to give herself the respect she deserved. Lizzy sat and looked into each person at her gathering, she was amazed to see the love that she was always surrounded by but couldn't see it, couldn't feel it, couldn't embrace it because her own heart was tainted with feelings of rejection.

"It was time to let go," Lizzy whispered looking up into the stars. Bill surprised her by asking, "let go of what?" Lizzy was surprised to see Bill standing in front of her. She felt whole again, with innocents, with love and with Bill holding hugging her tightly in his arms. As they walked back to the house, Lizzy knew this was true love and she absolutely deserved it.

We all deserve real love, we all deserve to have that one person embrace us. It's completely up to us to give into the healing of any situation. Once we come to terms with the fact that healing comes from the act of forgiving and moving forward we can all find true love. Learn to lose that emptiness, to erase the lust and fantasies of the thought of being in love. We can have it and we all are destined to it. But as Lizzy realized, we all must realize we have to come back to where it all started and begin again. Let go of the hurt, the pain, the tormented feelings of being worthless and move forward to another time. A new beginning of healing, with true family roots, true friends, laughter, trust and let go of the weight on your shoulders.

Lizzy sat for a moment and thanked God for the journey that had come to an end and the new beginning, a new chapter and one with great healing. She thought how it was her turn to be all the things she needed to be for herself and not all the things someone else needed her to be. She realized she had been great to everyone else, but not to herself. She learned a great lesson from her destructive behavior and it was that she needed to feel loved and not by someone else but by her own love.

Lizzy realized by the embrace and touch of Bill, hand in hand that love is a wonderful thing it heals all, it creates something in us that we can't experience otherwise. No amount of intimacy, lust or for the time being can ever replace the manifested feelings of true divine love. So, take a chance and love you, accept who you are, forgive and have no regrets. Finally, Bill turned to Lizzy and said I love you and she responded by saying I love me too.

Author:
Lisa Marie Dominguez

www.ingramcontent.com/pod-product-compliance
Lightning Source LLC
Chambersburg PA
CBHW041306110426
42743CB00037B/9